G000044196

TERRACE DESIGN

teNeues

Editor and texts: Alejandro Bahamón

Copy editing: Susana González

Layout: Ester Heredia

Translations: Jean Pierre Layre (French), Susanne Engler (German), Matthew Clarke (English), Maurizio Siliato (Italian)

Produced by Loft Publications
www.loftpublications.com

Published by teNeues Publishing Group

teNeues Publishing Company
16 West 22nd Street, New York, NY 10010, USA
Tel.: 001-212-627-9090, Fax: 001-212-627-9511

teNeues Book Division
Kaistraße 18
40221 Düsseldorf, Germany
Tel.: 0049-(0)211-994597-0, Fax: 0049-(0)211-994597-40

teNeues Publishing UK Ltd.
P.O. Box 402
West Byfleet
KT14 7ZF, Great Britain
Tel.: 0044-1932-403509, Fax: 0044-1932-403514

teNeues France S.A.R.L.
4, rue de Valence
75005 Paris, France
Tel.: 0033-1-55 76 62 05, Fax: 0033-1-55 76 64 19

www.teneues.com

ISBN: 3-8327-9041-1
Depósito Legal: B-21936-2005

© 2005 teNeues Verlag GmbH + Co. KG, Kempen

Printed in Spain

Bibliographic information published by
Die Deutsche Bibliothek. Die Deutsche Bibliothek lists
this publication in the Deutsche Nationalbibliografie;
detailed bibliographic data is available in the Internet
at http://dnb.ddb.de.

URBAN TERRACES

10–55

COUNTRYSIDE TERRACES

56–93

SEASIDE TERRACES

94–135

INTRODUCTION

EINLEITUNG

INTRODUCTION

INTRODUCCIÓN

INTRODUZIONE

The relationship between the exterior and interior is a determining factor in the personality of every home. Terraces are key elements when it comes to endowing living spaces with a deeper, more expansive and open quality. The earliest houses of all, temporary structures made with branches and animal skins, or even the cave dwellings had an outdoor area clearly defined as belonging to the home and in which important domestic activities were undertaken. It was the place for preparing food, cleaning, working and relaxing. Although today's homes are equipped to accommodate all these activities, the private outdoor area has been retained as an ideal spot for socializing and contemplation, as well as for the strong impression of expansiveness it bestows on the interior area. Over the course of this book, we offer a tour of the various possibilities for terrace design all over the world, in three chapters: urban terraces, country terraces and seaside terraces.

Die Beziehung, die in einem Wohnhaus zwischen außen und innen besteht, ist ein Faktor, der sich entscheidend auf den Charakter jeder Wohnung auswirkt. Terrassen sind Schlüsselelemente, wenn es darum geht, Wohnräume offener, tiefer und größer wirken zu lassen. Schon zu Zeiten der ersten Häuser, damals vergängliche Bauten aus Zweigen und Tierhäuten, oder sogar der Wohnhöhlen gab es immer schon einen klar definierten, äußeren Raum, der zum Wohnraum gehörte und in dem sich wichtige häusliche Aktivitäten abspielten. Dieser Ort diente der Zubereitung des Essens, der Reinigung, der Arbeit und der Freizeit. Obwohl die heutigen Wohnräume so ausgestattet sind, dass all diese Aktivitäten im Inneren stattfinden können, ist der private Raum im Freien immer noch ein idealer Ort für Zusammenkünfte und zum Entspannen, und er dient gleichzeitig dazu, das Gefühl von Weite in einem Haus oder einer Wohnung zu verstärken. In diesem Buch zeigen wir Ihnen verschiedene Gestaltungsmöglichkeiten für Terrassen auf der ganzen Welt, unterteilt in drei Kapitel: Terrassen in der Stadt, Terrassen auf dem Land und Terrassen am Meer.

La relation qu'il existe entre l'intérieur et l'extérieur d'un logement est un trait déterminant du caractère de chaque résidence. Les terrasses deviennent des pièces clés dès lors qu'il s'agit d'agrandir les espaces d'habitation, de les rendre plus profonds et plus ouverts. Depuis les origines de la maison, dans les constructions éphémères faites de branches et de peaux d'animaux ou dans les cavernes mêmes, il existait une zone extérieure clairement définie comme appartenant au logement et où on pratiquait les activités importantes de la maison. C'était l'endroit de la préparation des aliments, du nettoyage, du travail et des loisirs. Même si les logements contemporains sont aujourd'hui adaptés à la réalisation de toutes ces activités, on continue à profiter de cet espace extérieur privé comme d'un lieu de réunion, de contemplation où l'on peut avoir, grâce à lui une sensation d'espace intérieur accru. Tout au long de ce livre, on se propose de parcourir les différentes possibilités de design des terrasses dans le monde à travers trois chapitres : terrasses dans la ville, à la campagne et face à la mer.

La relación que existe entre el exterior y el interior de una vivienda es un rasgo determinante del carácter de cada residencia. Las terrazas se convierten en piezas clave para conseguir que los espacios logren una dimensión más amplia, profunda y abierta. Desde los mismos orígenes de la casa, construcciones efímeras hechas con ramas y pieles de animales o incluso en las propias cavernas, existía una zona exterior claramente definida como perteneciente a la vivienda y en donde se desarrollaban actividades importantes de la casa. Era el lugar de la preparación de alimentos, la limpieza, el trabajo y el ocio. Aunque las viviendas modernas están actualmente adaptadas a acoger todas estas actividades, se sigue manteniendo el espacio exterior privado como un lugar ideal de reunión, contemplación y por la sensación de amplitud que confiere al espacio interior. A lo largo de este libro se propone un recorrido de las diversas posibilidades de diseño de terrazas en el mundo dividido en tres capítulos: terrazas en la ciudad, en el campo y frente al mar.

© MONTSE GARRIGA

Il rapporto che esiste tra l'esterno e l'interno di un'abitazione è un tratto determinante del carattere di ogni costruzione. I terrazzi sono elementi chiave per far sì che gli spazi abitativi acquistino una dimensione più ampia, più profonda e aperta. Sin dalle stesse origini della casa, nelle costruzioni effimere fatte di rami e pelli di animali o persino nelle stesse caverne, esisteva una zona esterna i cui limiti definivano nettamente la sua appartenenza all'abitazione, e dove si svolgevano importanti attività domestiche. Questo era il luogo destinato a molteplici funzioni: preparazione degli alimenti, pulizia, lavoro e svago. Attualmente, sebbene le abitazioni contemporanee siano pronte ad accogliere nel loro interno tutte queste attività, si continua a mantenere lo spazio esterno privato come un luogo ideale di riunione e contemplazione, in grado anche di aumentare la sensazione di ampiezza degli interni. Questo volume propone un percorso illustrato lungo le diverse possibilità di progettazione e disegno di terrazzi in tutto il mondo. Il libro si divide in tre capitoli: terrazzi nelle città, in campagna e sul mare.

© MONTSE GARRIGA

Urban Terraces

Terrassen in der Stadt

Terrasses dans la ville

Terrazas en la ciudad

Terrazzi nelle città

© RAIMUND KOCH

City terraces, of whatever size, are perhaps the most introverted of all due to the density of the urban fabric, the closeness of neighbors and the unappealing views. This kind of designs, more than any other, seeks to hide eyesores, protect residents' privacy and provide a framework for the more interesting vistas available. As many such terraces are located on a roof, or simply because of the high price of real estate, they are areas of limited dimensions. However, it is also possible to find terraces in family houses bordered by a large garden. These tend to be slightly larger and resemble country terraces, although there is always the conditioning factor of limited views. In other cases, when a terrace is set on a roof or the top floors of high buildings, panoramic views of the city are on offer, making it similar to a seaside terrace. In the urban context, elements intended to control privacy, pergolas or trellises, for example, take on a vital importance and they develop a very close relationship with the architecture of the adjoining building. These terraces also use vegetation, such as hedges and thick shrubs, as a protective barrier.

Stadtterrassen, egal ob klein oder groß, sind aufgrund der dichten Besiedlung der Städte, der Nähe zu den Nachbarn und der teilweise nicht besonders schönen Aussichten eher in sich geschlossene Räume. Bei der Gestaltung von Stadtterrassen wird oft versucht, einen weniger schönen Anblick zu verstecken, die Privatsphäre der Bewohner zu schützen und einen interessanten Ausblick zu unterstreichen. Da sich viele dieser Terrassen auf dem Dach befinden oder die Grundstückspreise sehr hoch sind, sind sie oft sehr klein. Es gibt jedoch auch Terrassen in Einfamilienhäusern, die in einen großen Garten führen. Diese Art von Terrassen ist weiträumig angelegt und gleicht denen auf dem Lande, obwohl auch hier der Blick oft eingeschränkt ist. Dann wiederum gibt es Terrassen, die auf einem Dach oder in den oberen Geschossen liegen, so dass man einen wundervollen Blick auf die Stadt hat. Sie gleichen Terrassen am Meer. Für Stadtterrassen sind Elemente wie Pergolen oder Gitter, die die Privatsphäre schützen, von großer Bedeutung. Auch die Beziehung zu dem Gebäude, auf oder an dem sie sich befinden, darf niemals außer Acht gelassen werden. Die Vegetation, z. B. Hecken oder Büsche mit dichtem Laubwerk, dient in diesen Fällen auch als eine schützende Barriere.

Les terrasses à l'intérieur des villes, qu'elles soient grandes ou petites, sont peut-être les plus discrètes de par la densité urbaine, le voisinage proche ou les vis-à-vis indésirables. Plus que pour les autres, le design des terrasses en ville, cherche à cacher les vues les moins favorables, à protéger l'intimité des habitants et à servir de cadre aux vues les plus intéressantes. Beaucoup de terrasses se trouvant sur des toits plats ou simplement à cause du prix élevé des terrains, il s'agit d'espaces aux proportions réduites. Cependant il existe aussi des terrasses dans des maisons individuelles qui ont un grand jardin. Dans ce cas précis, elles sont un peu plus étendues et arrivent à ressembler beaucoup aux terrasses des maisons à la campagne, même si elles restent soumises à des panoramas restreints. Autre exemple : celui des terrasses se trouvant sur un toit plat ou à des étages élevés dans des bâtiments, permettant de profiter de larges vues sur la ville et qui, dans ce cas, s'apparentent à celles se trouvant face à la mer. Sur les terrasses en ville, les éléments contribuant à l'intimité comme les pergolas ou les grillages sont d'une importance vitale et leur rapport à l'architecture du bâtiment où ils se trouvent est très étroit. Dans ces cas précis, la végétation, comme les haies et arbustes à feuillage dense, est utilisée comme barrière protectrice.

Las terrazas que se encuentran en las ciudades, por pequeñas o grandes que sean, son quizás las más introvertidas debido a la densidad urbana, la cercanía de vecinos o las vistas indeseables. El diseño de estas terrazas, más que ningún otro, busca ocultar las vistas menos favorables, proteger la privacidad de los habitantes y enmarcar las panorámicas más interesantes. Puesto que muchas se encuentran en azoteas, o simplemente debido al alto precio del suelo, se trata de espacios de reducidas proporciones. Sin embargo, también existen terrazas en viviendas unifamiliares que cuentan con un amplio jardín. En estos casos son un poco más amplias y se parecen mucho a las terrazas en el campo, aunque siempre existe la condicionante de las panorámicas limitadas. En otras ocasiones, cuando la terraza se encuentra en una azotea o en plantas muy elevadas de un edificio, permiten disfrutar amplias vistas de la ciudad y entonces se asemejan a las que se encuentran junto al mar. En las terrazas en la ciudad son de vital importancia los elementos para controlar la privacidad, como pérgolas o rejas, y su relación con la arquitectura del edificio en donde se encuentran es muy estrecha. La vegetación, en estos casos, se utiliza también como barrera protectora, como los setos y arbustos de denso follaje.

I terrazzi costruiti all'interno di città, per quanto piccole o grandi queste siano, sono forse quelli più introversi a causa della densità urbana, la vicinanza dei vicini o di viste indesiderabili. Nella misura del possibile, i terrazzi urbani vengono progettati in modo tale da proteggere la privacy degli abitanti, nascondere le vedute meno piacevoli e mettere in risalto quelle più interessanti. Visto che molti terrazzi occupano i ripiani di copertura degli edifici, o semplicemente per l'elevato prezzo del terreno, si tratta di spazi di dimensioni ridotte. In alcune abitazioni unifamiliari esistono comunque terrazzi dotati inoltre di un ampio giardino. In questo caso i terrazzi sono leggermente più grandi e molto simili a quelli delle costruzioni di campagna, anche se le viste panoramiche sono limitate. Nei casi di terrazze che occupano i piani alti degli edifici, questi elementi consentono di godere di ampie viste panoramiche della città e sono simili ai terrazzi costruiti accanto al mare. Nei terrazzi di città sono di vitale importanza gli elementi che servono a controllare la privacy, come pergolati o reti, e il loro rapporto con l'architettura dell'edificio dove sono situate è molto stretto. In questi casi, la vegetazione si utilizza pure come barriera di protezione, sotto forma di siepi e arbusti dal fogliame fitto.

Wooden trusses, both vertical and horizontal, are very useful elements in city terraces as they not only provide a degree of intimacy but also serve as a structure for some climbing plants.

Vertikales und horizontales Flechtwerk aus Holz ist ein nützliches Element für Stadtterrassen, da es von den Nachbarn abschirmt und gleichzeitig als Struktur für Kletterpflanzen dient.

Les treillages en bois, qu'ils soient placés en position verticale ou horizontale, sont des éléments très utiles sur les terrasses de ville car d'une part, ils leur confèrent d'eux-mêmes une certaine intimité et d'autre part, ils servent de structure pour certaines plantes grimpantes.

Los entramados de madera, tanto verticales como horizontales, son elementos muy útiles en las terrazas urbanas, ya que otorgan cierta intimidad por sí solas y a la vez sirven como estructura para ciertas plantas enredaderas.

I graticci di legno, sia quelli verticali che orizzontali, sono elementi molto utili nei terrazzi urbani visto che non sono offrono una certa privacy ma servono inoltre come struttura di sostegno per le piante rampicanti.

The large windows between the home's interior and the terrace accentuate the link between the two spaces: the terrace becomes one more room belonging to the house, while the interior takes on a much more expansive dimension.

Die großen Fenster zwischen der Wohnung und der Terrasse verbinden die beiden Räume. So wird die Terrasse zu einem weiteren Wohnraum und die Innenräume wirken viel weiter.

Les grandes baies vitrées qui se trouvent entre l'intérieur du logement et la terrasse accentuent le lien existant entre ces deux espaces. La terrasse devient d'une part une pièce supplémentaire de la maison, d'autre part l'espace intérieur gagne en dimension.

Los grandes ventanales entre el espacio interior de la vivienda y la terraza acentúan el vínculo entre estos dos ámbitos. Por una parte, la terraza se convierte en una estancia más de la casa, mientras que el espacio interior adquiere una dimensión mucho más amplia.

I grandi finestroni tra lo spazio interno dell'abitazione e il terrazzo accentuano il legame tra questi due ambienti. Da una parte il terrazzo si trasforma in un'altra stanza, mentre l'interno acquisisce una dimensione molto più ampia.

© Kouji Okamoto

© Peter Clarke

small wall or low trellis with plants serves to provide total privacy in terra-
s set on the top floor of a building. The view of the sky takes on great
portance and a very intimate setting can be created.

e kleine, niedrige Mauer oder ein niedriges Flechtwerk aus Pflanzen sor-
n auf den Terrassen der oberen Etagen für Privatsphäre. Der Blick zum
mmel wird betont und die Atmosphäre wirkt sehr intim.

petit mur bas ou un treillage végétal de faible hauteur sont des éléments
i proportionnent une intimité totale aux terrasses situées aux derniers
ages d'un bâtiment. La vue dégagée sur le ciel en devient l'élément princi-
l et permet de créer une atmosphère très personnelle.

pequeño muro bajo, o un entramado vegetal de poca altura, sirve como
mento que otorga total privacidad cuando se trata de terrazas ubicadas
las últimas plantas de un edificio. La vista hacia el cielo adquiere gran pro-
gonismo y se logra un ambiente muy íntimo.

lle terrazze di copertura che occupano gli ultimi piani degli edifici, a volte
sta solo un piccolo muro, o un graticcio vegetale per fungere da elementi
isori e dare allo spazio l'apposita privacy. In questo modo si ottiene un
nbiente molto intimo, ideale per ammirare il cielo sovrastante.

© MONTSE GARRIGA

© MONTSE GARRIGA

© MONTSE GARRIGA

© MONTSE GARRIGA

me single-family **homes are** surrounded by a large garden, which is ideal
shutting out **neighbours** and urban congestion in general. The presence
more substantial **vegetation** defines both the limits and the nature of the
race.

anche Einfamilienhäuser haben einen großen Garten, der sie von den
chbarn und dem städtischen Trubel trennt. Größere Pflanzen definieren
Grenzen und den Charakter der Terrasse.

ville, certaines maisons particulières ont un grand jardin tout autour qui
t à les isoler naturellement des voisins et de la vie urbaine en général.
uvoir y planter une végétation dense définit les limites et le caractère de
errasse.

rtas viviendas unifamiliares cuentan con un amplio jardín circundante
e sirve como aislante de vecinos cercanos y la congestión urbana en gene-
La presencia de una vegetación de mayor porte define los límites y el
ácter de la terraza.

une abitazioni unifamiliari dispongono, all'intorno, di un ampio giardino
e serve in genere per isolare gli edifici dai vicini e dalla congestione urba-
La presenza di una **vegetazione** più copiosa definisce i limiti e il carattere
terrazzo.

© MONTSE GARRIGA

© MONTSE GARRIGA

© JORDI MIRALLES

Countryside Terraces

Terrassen auf dem Land

Terrasses à la campagne

Terrazas en el campo

Terrazzi in campagna

In rural areas, the tendency to inhabit spaces outside the house becomes more apparent. Many activities typical of a country home, such as looking after plants, picking fruit and, in many cases, rearing animals, demand living spaces that are set outdoors. Furthermore, the big available land makes it possible to design very large terraces that blend in with a garden and the surrounding landscape. Country terraces thereby become not mere extensions of interiors but rooms in their own right, such as lounges, play areas, dining rooms and even cooking areas. The furniture becomes more complete and the design, generally marked by the surroundings, take on a pronounced rustic look. The design of the architectural elements that form such terraces as well as that of the furnishings and decorative details demands great resistance and durability, so it turns to materials such as stone, ceramics, wood and metal. Vegetation also plays a major role, as regards not only the plants chosen for the terrace itself but also the lushness offered by the surrounding natural landscape. The possibility of putting plants and small trees directly into the earth creates a very close relationship with nature.

In ländlichen Gegenden werden die Außenanlagen der Häuser sehr gerne als zusätzlicher Wohnraum genutzt. Rund ums Landhaus fallen viele Aktivitäten wie das Pflanzen, Ernten und die Tierhaltung an, so dass viele Bereiche im Freien benötigt werden. Zudem lässt die Größe des Grundstücks die Gestaltung großer Terrassen zu, die in den Garten und die umgebende Landschaft übergehen. Terrassen auf dem Land sind deshalb keine bloßen Erweiterungen der Innenräume, sondern sie sind eigene Räume wie Wohn- und Spielzimmer, Speisezimmer und sogar Küchen. Sie sind oft komplett möbliert und im Einklang mit der Umgebung rustikal gestaltet. Bei den architektonischen Elementen, den Möbeln und den Dekorationselementen wird nach Haltbarkeit und Widerstandsfähigkeit gesucht, so dass gerne Materialien wie Stein, Keramik, Holz oder Metall eingesetzt werden. Auf diesen Terrassen spielt die Vegetation eine entscheidende Rolle, dies betrifft nicht nur die Pflanzen, die sich auf der Terrasse selbst befinden, sondern auch die umgebende Natur. Da Blumen, Büsche und kleine Bäume direkt in die Erde gepflanzt werden können, wird die Beziehung zur Natur viel enger.

Dans les zones rurales, il est beaucoup plus habituel d'habiter les parties extérieures de la maison. En effet, les multiples activités pratiquées dans ce type de lieu, comme le jardinage, les récoltes des fruits, ou dans la plupart des cas l'élevage des animaux, font que de nombreuses pièces de la maison sont situées à l'extérieur. D'autre part, la grandeur du terrain disponible permet de concevoir des terrasses plus grandes, qui se fondent dans le jardin et le paysage environnant. Ces terrasses ne sont plus alors des extensions d'intérieurs du logement mais des pièces propres à la maison, comme des salons, des zones de jeu, des salles à manger et même des endroits où l'on cuisine. Leur mobilier est plus complet et le design, en général influencé par l'environnement où elles se trouvent, a un style rustique très prononcé. Les éléments architecturaux qui les composent, tout comme le mobilier et les détails décoratifs, cherchent une plus grande résistance et durabilité en utilisant des matériaux comme la pierre, la céramique, le bois ou le métal. Sur ce type de terrasse, la végétation présente mais aussi celle de l'environnement naturel jouent le rôle principal. De plus, paysager le terrain permet d'établir une relation étroite avec la nature.

En las áreas rurales la tendencia a habitar las zonas exteriores de la casa se hace muy presente. Este tipo de viviendas desarrolla actividades como el cuidado de las plantas, la recolección de frutas o en muchos casos la cría de animales, que hacen que muchas de las estancias de la vivienda estén en el exterior. Por otra parte, la gran extensión de la que disponen permite diseñar terrazas muy amplias que se confunden con el jardín y el paisaje circundante. Estas terrazas se convierten ya no en extensiones de los interiores de la vivienda, sino en estancias propias de la casa, como salones, zonas de juego, comedores y hasta áreas de cocina. El mobiliario se hace más completo y el diseño, por lo general marcado por el entorno en donde se encuentran, tiene un marcado acento rústico. El diseño de los elementos arquitectónicos que la componen, así como del mobiliario y los detalles decorativos, busca una gran resistencia y durabilidad, por lo que se recurre a materiales como la piedra, la cerámica, la madera o el metal. En este tipo de terrazas la vegetación tiene un papel protagonista, no sólo por la proyectada en la misma terraza sino por la profanidad que supone en el paisaje natural circundante. La posibilidad de sembrar plantas y pequeños árboles directamente sobre el terreno permite una relación muy estrecha con la naturaleza.

Nelle zone rurali la tendenza ad abitare gli spazi esterni della casa è ancora più evidente. In questo tipo di abitazioni, sono molte le attività che si possono realizzare, come per esempio: prendersi cura delle piante, la raccolta della frutta e in molti casi allevare animali, e fanno sì che molti ambienti della casa si situino all'esterno. Tra l'altro, l'estensione di cui godone permettono di progettare terrazzi molto ampi, che si confondono con il giardino e il paesaggio circostante. Questi terrazzi non sono semplici prolungamenti degli interni bensì dei vani veri e propri, come saloni, zone gioco, sale da pranzo e persino zone cucina. L'ambiente influisce decisamente sui mobili da usare per arredare questi spazi; di solito si tende a utilizzare una mobilia dalle marcate linee rustiche. In generale, il disegno degli elementi architettonici, così come dei mobili e dei particolari decorativi tende a una gran resistenza e durabilità, per questo si ricorre a materiali come la pietra, la ceramica, il legno o il metallo. In questo tipo di terrazzi, la rigogliosa vegetazione assume un ruolo da protagonista. Infatti, la possibilità di piantare piccoli arbusti e piante direttamente sul terreno incrementa ulteriormente lo stretto rapporto con la natura.

ting a house in the middle of a wood provides the ideal opportunity for
nting a garden without borders, in which the terrace serves as a link be-
een the natural wilderness and the interior. A simple platform floating on
land contrasts with the exuberant vegetation.

Haus mitten im Wald ist der ideale Ort, um einen Garten ohne Grenzen
zulegen, in dem die Terrasse als Bindeglied zwischen der wilden Natur
d dem Inneren dient. Eine einfache Plattform, die über dem Gelände
webt, bildet einen Gegensatz zu der üppigen Vegetation.

nstruire une maison au milieu d'un bois est une occasion idéale pour
nter un jardin sans limite, où la terrasse remplit sa fonction de lien entre
ure sauvage et intérieur. Une simple plate-forme flottante sur le terrain
traste avec la végétation exubérante.

icar una casa en medio de un bosque es la oportunidad idónea para plan-
r un jardín sin límites, en donde la terraza cumple la función de vínculo
re naturaleza agreste e interior. Una simple plataforma que flota sobre el
reno contrasta con la exuberante vegetación.

cidere di edificare una casa in mezzo a un bosco è l'opportunità ideale per
dere sempre di un giardino senza limiti, dove il terrazzo funge da vincolo
la natura agreste e l'interno dell'abitazione. Una semplice piattaforma
eggiante sul terreno contrasta con l'esuberante vegetazione.

In tropical climates, where the temperatures are high throughout the year, terraces play a fundamental role in the design of single-family homes. They represent not only extensions to the house but also a sequence of spaces related to the exterior.

In tropischen Gebieten, in denen immer hohe Temperaturen herrschen, sind Terrassen ein grundlegender Bestandteil von Einfamilienhäusern. Sie sind nicht nur eine Verlängerung des Hauses, sondern eine Sequenz von Räumen, die mit draußen in Verbindung stehen.

Sous des climats tropicaux, où toute l'année les températures sont toujours élevées, les terrasses font partie intégrante du design des maisons particulières. Ce sont non seulement des extensions de la maison, mais aussi une suite de pièces liées à l'extérieur.

En climas tropicales, en donde a lo largo de todo el año las temperaturas son siempre elevadas, las terrazas forman parte fundamental en el diseño de viviendas unifamiliares. No sólo son extensiones de la casa, también funcionan como una secuencia de estancias relacionadas con el exterior.

Nelle zone con clima tropicale, dove per tutto l'anno le temperature sono sempre elevate, i terrazzi sono parte essenziale della struttura di molte abitazioni unifamiliari. Non si tratta soltanto di semplici prolungamenti della casa ma di una successione di vani e ambienti in stretto legame con l'esterno.

hen the lay of the land allows it, and the house is to be set on the top of a
ll, the terrace can serve as a veritable vantage point. A simple platform
th few furnishings is sufficient to set off the panoramic views of the
ndscape.

enn die Geländeform es zulässt und das Haus oben auf einem Hügel
:ht, werden Terrassen auf dem Lande zu wahren Aussichtspunkten. Eine
ıfache Plattform und wenig Möbel reichen aus, um die Aufmerksamkeit
f den Ausblick zu lenken.

land la topographie le permet, que la maison peut être construite en haut
ıne colline, les terrasses peuvent devenir de véritables miradors. Une sim-
: plate-forme et très peu de mobilier suffisent à ce que les vues sur le pay-
ge se détachent.

ando la topografía lo permite, y la vivienda puede ubicarse en la parte alta
una colina, las terrazas se pueden convertirse en verdaderos miradores.
a sencilla plataforma y poco mobiliario son suficientes para destacar las
norámicas del paisaje.

ando la topografia lo permette, ed è possibile costruire le abitazioni nella
rte alta di una collina, i terrazzi possono diventare veri e propri belvedere.
sta solo una semplice piattaforma in legno e pochi mobili, ad abbellire il
tto ci pensa il paesaggio circostante.

e protection of furniture is of vital importance on some terraces. A light
of, made of beams and wooden canes, serves as a gentle filter against the
ht, as well as helping to protect the furniture and create a more intimate
d secluded setting.

f manchen Terrassen ist es wichtig, die Möbel zu schützen. Ein leichtes
ch, z. B. aus Holzbalken oder Holzstäben, wirkt wie ein leichter Filter gegen
s Sonnenlicht. Es schützt die Möbel und schafft eine intime, gemütliche
mosphäre.

otéger le mobilier de certaines terrasses est parfois très important. Une
gère couverture, des poutres en bois et des canisses, servent à filtrer la
mière, protège le mobilier et créent une atmosphère intime et douillette.

protección del mobiliario en ciertas terrazas es de fundamental importan-
. Una cubierta ligera, por ejemplo de vigas y cáñamos de madera, sirve
mo suave filtro de la luz, protege el mobiliario y crea una atmósfera íntima
ecogida.

alcuni terrazzi la questione della protezione dei mobili è di fondamentale
portanza. Una copertura leggera, fatta per esempio di canapa o di travi in
no, serve da soave filtro alla luce, protegge i mobili e crea un'atmosfera
ima e raccolta.

© JORDI MIRALLES

© JORDI MIRALLES

© UNDINE PRÖHL

©UNDINE PRÖHL

art from swimming pools, water can be used in the form of small ponds
create mirrors of water. Its presence not only incorporates an additional
tural element into the terrace but also helps to mark out the space and
eate a relaxing effect.

asser kann nicht nur in Form von Swimmingpools, sondern auch in kleinen
chen eingesetzt werden, um spiegelnde Flächen zu erzeugen. Es ist nicht
r ein weiteres natürliches Element auf der Terrasse, sondern es begrenzt
ch den Raum und wirkt entspannend.

plus des piscines, l'eau peut être utilisée en guise de petits étangs pour
er des miroirs d'eau. Elle offre non seulement un élément naturel supplé-
entaire à la terrasse mais aussi elle aide à délimiter l'espace et crée un effet
axant.

emás de las piscinas, el agua puede ser empleada en forma de pequeños
tanques para crear espejos de agua. Su presencia no sólo incorpora un ele-
ento natural adicional a la terraza, sino que ayuda a delimitar el espacio y
ea un efecto relajante.

questi terrazzi la applicazioni dell'acqua sono molteplici: principalmente
tto forma di piscina, ma anche di piccoli laghetti per creare specchi d'ac-
a. La sua presenza non solo aggiunge un ulteriore elemento naturale al
rrazzo ma aiuta pure a delimitare lo spazio creando un effetto rilassante.

The distant horizon, the expansive panoramas, the absence of close neighbors and the predominance of the blue sea are the main features of these terraces, which tend to have a marked horizontality in their design. Furthermore, they are generally outdoor spaces that need to be protected from weather conditions, such as burning sunshine, the presence of salt in the atmosphere and strong winds. As a result, the materials most often found on these terraces are those that adapt best to these conditions. Metal must be specially treated against corrosion. Stone can be very slippery in some cases, due to the effect of salt and water, while glass requires a great deal of maintenance, although it is often the ideal option for combining protection from the wind with unimpeded enjoyment of the views. Wood seems to be the most appropriate material for this type of terrace, however, on account of its resistance against water and wind. Depending on the house's location with respect to the sea front, these terraces can create such an effect of depth that the interior itself comes to be seen as part of the exterior space. The climatic conditions also affect the choice of vegetation, which is generally confined to indigenous species.

Diese Art von Terrassen wird vom Horizont, dem wundervollen Ausblick, der Abwesenheit nächster Nachbarn und dem Blau des Meeres geprägt und wird betont horizontal angelegt. Allerdings sind sie auch Außenräume, die vor Klimaeinflüssen wie der starken Sonneneinstrahlung, dem Salz in der Luft und den starken Winden geschützt werden müssen. Deshalb werden auf diesen Terrassen Materialien verwendet, die diesen Klimaeinflüssen standhalten. So muss zum Beispiel Metall mit speziellen Korrosionsschutzmitteln behandelt werden. Steine können durch Salz und Wasser manchmal sehr rutschig werden. Glas benötigt viel Pflege, obwohl es auch das ideale Material ist, um vor Wind zu schützen und trotzdem den schönen Blick zu erhalten. Holz ist aufgrund seiner Eignung für Wind und Wasser das beste Material für diese Art von Terrassen. Je nach Lage des Hauses zum Meer hin können diese Terrassen eine Tiefe schaffen, die dazu führt, dass die Innenräume wie Außenräume wirken. Das Klima beeinflusst auch die Vegetation, die normalerweise nur aus einheimischen Arten besteht.

L'horizon, les vues dégagées, l'absence de voisins aux alentours et la couleur bleu marine prédominante sont les principales caractéristiques de ces terrasses marquées par un design horizontal. Par ailleurs ce sont des espaces extérieurs qu'il faut généralement protéger des intempéries, du soleil intense, de la présence de sel dans l'atmosphère ou des vents violents. De ce fait, les matériaux les plus utilisés pour ces terrasses sont ceux qui s'adaptent le mieux à ces conditions atmosphériques. Le métal doit être spécialement traité contre la corrosion. La pierre peut parfois se révéler très glissante à cause du sel et de l'eau. Alors que le verre, qui pourtant nécessite beaucoup d'entretien, est bien souvent la solution idéale, à la fois pour se protéger du vent et pour apprécier la vue panoramique. Le bois, grâce à ses qualités de résistance à l'eau et au vent, semble être le matériau le plus approprié pour ce type de terrasse. Selon la situation de la maison par rapport au front de mer, ces terrasses peuvent créer un tel effet de profondeur que l'on arrive à ressentir l'intérieur comme partie intégrante de l'extérieur. Les conditions climatiques influent aussi sur le type de végétation choisie, se réduisant généralement à des espèces indigènes.

El horizonte, las amplias panorámicas, la ausencia de vecinos cercanos y el predominante azul marino son las principales características de estas terrazas, que tienen una marcada tendencia horizontal en su diseño. Por otra parte, son espacios exteriores que generalmente hay que proteger de las inclemencias del tiempo, como el intenso sol, la presencia de sal en el ambiente o los fuertes vientos. Por eso los materiales más presentes en estas terrazas son los que mejor se adaptan a estas condiciones ambientales. El metal debe someterse a tratamientos anticorrosivos específicos. La piedra puede resultar en algunos casos muy resbaladiza por el efecto de la sal y el agua, mientras que el cristal requiere de mucho mantenimiento, aunque en muchos casos es la solución ideal para protegerse del viento y continuar disfrutando de la panorámica. La madera, por sus cualidades frente al agua y el viento, parece ser el material más apropiado para este tipo de terrazas. En función de la situación de la casa con respecto al frente marítimo, estas terrazas pueden crear un efecto de tal profundidad que se llega a percibir el propio interior como parte del exterior. Las condiciones climáticas afectan también al tipo de vegetación, que generalmente se reduce a especies autóctonas.

L'orizzonte, le vaste vedute panoramiche, l'assenza di vicini a poca distanza, e il predominante blu del mare sono le principali caratteristiche di questi terrazzi le cui linee presentano una marcata orizzontalità. Generalmente si tratta di spazi esterni che vanno protetti dalle inclemenze del tempo, come il sole intenso, la presenza di salsedine nell'ambiente o i forti venti. Per questo motivo i materiali più utilizzati in questi terrazzi sono quelli che più si adattano alle difficili condizioni ambientali. Il metallo deve essere sottoposto a uno specifico trattamento anticorrosivo. In alcuni casi la pietra può risultare molto scivolosa per l'effetto della salsedine e dell'acqua mentre il vetro ha bisogno di molta manutenzione, sebbene in molti casi rimane la soluzione ideale per proteggersi dal vento e continuare a godere del panorama. Il legno, per le sua resistenza all'acqua e al vento, sembra essere il materiale più appropriato per questo tipo di terrazzi. In base alla posizione della casa rispetto al litorale marittimo, questi terrazzi possono creare un effetto di profondità tale da far percepire gli interni come parte dell'esterno. Le condizioni climatiche incidono anche sul tipo di vegetazione, che in genere si riduce a specie autoctone.

layout of the swimming pool, as well as its size and shape, plays a cru-
role in this type of terrace. In many cases, it serves as an element that
ks out the exterior space while also accentuating the horizontality pro-
d by the panoramic view of the sea.

Position, die Form und die Größe des Swimmingpools spielen eine
ndlegende Rolle bei dieser Art von Terrassen. Oft wird durch den Swim-
gpool der äußere Raum begrenzt und gleichzeitig die Horizontale, die
ch den Blick aufs Meer entsteht, unterstrichen.

isposition de la piscine, tout comme sa forme et sa taille, joue un rôle
important dans ce type de terrasse. Elle sert très souvent à délimiter
ace extérieur et, en même temps, à accentuer l'horizontalité qu'offre la
dégagée vers la mer.

isposición de la piscina, así como su forma y tamaño, desempeñan un
el crucial en este tipo de terrazas. En muchos casos sirve como elemento
delimita el espacio exterior y al mismo tiempo acentúa la horizontalidad
ofrece la panorámica del mar.

isposizione della piscina, così come la sua forma e le sue dimensioni,
gono un ruolo cruciale in questo tipo di terrazzi. In molti casi, la piscina
e concepito come un elemento che delimita lo spazio esterno e al con-
oo serve per accentuare l'orizzontalità data dalla vista panoramica del
e.

© ENRIQUE BROWNE

© RICARDO LABOUGLE

less benign climates, it is necessary to cover several sides of the terrace, including the top, in order to protect it from the strong winds and heavy rain that lash some coastlines. These conditions require unfussy, resistant furniture.

i rauhem Klima ist es notwendig, mehrere Seiten der Terrasse abzuschirmen oder sie zu überdachen, um vor den starken Winden und heftigem gen zu schützen, die oft an der Küste aufkommen. Unter diesen klimatischen Bedingungen muss das Mobiliar schlicht und widerstandsfähig sein.

us des latitudes moins favorables, il faut couvrir plusieurs côtés de la terasse, y compris la partie supérieure, afin de la protéger des vents forts ou s pluies intenses qui s'abattent sur certains littoraux. Dans ces conditions, n mobilier sobre et résistant est nécessaire.

n climas menos favorables es necesario cubrir varios costados de la terraza, cluso la parte superior, con el objetivo de protegerla de los fuertes vientos las intensas lluvias que azotan ciertos litorales. En estas condiciones se ace necesario un mobiliario austero y resistente.

certe zone dove le condizioni climatiche non sono favorevoli, occorre coprivari lati del terrazzo, persino la parte superiore, al fine di proteggerlo dai rti venti o dalle intense piogge che si abbattono su certi litorali. In queste ndizioni è opportuno usare degli elementi di arredo semplici e resistenti.

© PETER COOK / VIEW

© PETER COOK / VIEW

© Ron Dahlquist

© Ron Dahlquist

© Ron Dahlquist

chitectural elements such as pergolas, partial roofs and awnings are major ources when it comes to designing these terraces and protecting them m the sun. The arrangement of these elements makes it possible to play ch the compositions created by the shadows over the course of the day.

chitektonische Elemente wie Pergolen, Teilüberdachungen oder Markisen d Schlüsselelemente, um die Terrassen vor der Sonne zu schützen. Die ordnung dieser Elemente erlaubt eine Komposition des Schattenspiels im ufe des Tages.

ns le design de ces terrasses, on peut recourir à des éléments d'architec-e comme les pergolas, les couvertures partielles ou les stores pour les pro-ger du soleil. La disposition de ces éléments permet de jouer avec la com-sition produite par les ombres tout au long de la journée.

mentos arquitectónicos como pérgolas, cubiertas parciales o toldos son ursos importantes en el diseño de estas terrazas para protegerlas del sol. disposición de estos elementos permite jugar con la composición que pro-cen las sombras a lo largo del día.

fine di proteggere molti terrazzi dal sole vengono usati alcuni elementi hitettonici quali pergole, coperture parziali o tende. La disposizione di esti elementi permette giocare con la composizione prodotta dalle ombre corso della giornata.

© ALEJO BAGUE

© ALEJO BAGUE

©ALEJO BAGUE

ood is the preferred option on this type of terrace, for both the furniture d exterior finishing, as its surface is resistant, durable and non-slip. Al-ough it requires frequent maintenance, its ageing integrates it into the astal landscape.

uf diesen Terrassen ist Holz das beliebteste Material, sowohl für die Möbel s auch für die Oberflächen. Holz ist rutschfest, widerstandsfähig und halt-r. Obwohl Holz eine häufige Instandhaltung benötigt, passt sich das ernde Holz gut in die Küstenlandschaft ein.

bois est le matériau préféré dans ce type de terrasses, aussi bien pour le obilier que pour les finitions extérieures, car c'est une superficie antidéra-nte, résistante et durable. Même s'il faut l'entretenir régulièrement, il s'in-gre parfaitement dans le paysage maritime en vieillissant.

madera es el material preferido en este tipo de terrazas, tanto para el obiliario como en los acabados exteriores, pues es una superficie antides-ante, resistente y duradera. Aunque requiere un mantenimiento frecuen-su envejecimiento se integra con el paisaje marino.

azie alle sua resistenza, durabilità e proprietà antiscivolo, il legno è il mate-le preferito in questo tipo di terrazzi, sia per i mobili che per le finiture terne. Sebbene richieda una frequente manutenzione, il suo aspetto invec-iato si integra con il paesaggio marino.

© JORDI MIRALLES

© UNDINE PRÖHL

© MONTSE GARRIGA